—

FAMILY BUDGET
For Beginners

**Everything You Want To Know
About Family Budget Planning**

Gemma Brooks

Table Of Contents

Money Saving Tips: Where To Begin

In this article we will look at the reasons for putting money aside and discuss some methods in to get started. We will also look at clever ways to reduce spending in several areas of your life. By following the advice given in this article, you will be well on your way to cutting your expenditures and having more in your bank account.

Where to Begin

When it comes to saving money, many people have no idea where to begin. The vast majority of people in the USA don't even know how much they have in their bank, savings or checking accounts. How many times have you asked yourself, where does it all go? Finding out is easy and essential if you're ever going to turn things around.

Computer companies make millions on expensive software guaranteed to organize your finances for you. The first money saving tip you can put into practice is giving all of those a total miss. Instead of spending 200 dollars on computer software, spend 5 on a notebook and a pack of pens. All that is needed to get started is some simple bookkeeping.

Once you have your equipment, take 2 weeks and write down everything that you spend. It doesn't matter how insignificant the expense seems, it must be listed. Carry this notebook with you at all times.

You may forget to list something, especially if it is small which will throw off your total amount of expenditure. Once the two weeks has ended, you will see where all of your money is going. You may be surprised and shocked to see how much actually goes on frivolous and insignificant items.

Many who practice this exercise find it quite upsetting but also quite sobering. They also find that once they know where all their money is going, it is easy to implement a plan for change.

Saving money isn't difficult and doesn't require expensive gadgets. All you need is to find out where your money is going which required only time.

Set Up a Family Budget for Every Member of the Family

One thing that parents often hear as their child nears adolescence is "Can I have some money?" Children want things much the same way adults do. Things like trips to the movies, CDs, or a new skateboard. For a child who is too young to have a job, their parent often becomes the source for their spending.

When you set a family budget it's important to include your children's needs as well. It's crucial though to differentiate between needs and wants. All children want things and parents enjoy giving those things to their children. But an endless supply of requests for money can quickly break any parent's budget in two.

If you child wants things that weren't included when you set a family budget there are a few things you can do:

Make a chore jar for older children. This is a jar that contains extra jobs and the amounts you are offering for them. This is separate from the child's regular daily list of chores and can include items such as painting the fence or washing the car.

Create a bank account for your child and deposit any Christmas or birthday money they receive. If you do this, when your child really desires something during the year you can check the account balance and then explain to them whether or not they have enough to budget for the item. If they don't they can work extra chores to make up the difference or wait until another birthday or special event passes.

Placing a bit of money aside when you set a family budget, for your child is a good idea, but it's important to make certain that they work for that money. Giving a child everything they desire is lovely in theory but it doesn't teach them that a budget is essential to financial success.

Teach Your Children The Value Of A Dime

When children are small they are usually excited to find a penny under the sofa cushion or to be presented with a dime when they've helped with a small task. This fascination with money can quickly fade and children lose track of what it means to save.

When you sit down with your spouse or partner to set a family budget, it's wise to include your children in part of the process. Children don't need to know the details about mortgage costs or insurance premiums, but they can be included in certain aspects of household financial planning.

Teaching your children the value of a dollar isn't really that difficult. Children understand at a fairly young age that in order to purchase things you need to pay for them. They watch their parents open their wallets and remove money or a credit card to purchase everything from grocery items to toys. They understand that mommy or daddy had to go to work to make that money.

Giving a child a list of chores to complete and a value for each one helps them see that with hard work comes reward. The chores don't have to be complicated, for young children it can be something as simple as picking up their toys or setting the dinner table. They will feel the reward of a dollar earned when they are able to take that money to the store and purchase something they really want.

Setting time aside to set a household budget is a great idea and incorporating everyone's contributions to the home is important. Placing a small amount of money aside for your children's allowance each month will give them a great head start for their own budgeting needs later in life.

Children Can Save Too

To set a family budget takes a good deal of patience along with some careful planning. When you've got children the process can be even more extensive. Planning for things like their medical coverage, college needs and perhaps eventual wedding plans all need to be taken into consideration.

A parent can set a family budget that includes a savings account for their child and this can begin even before the child is born. Savings can never begin too young and each dollar you save will directly benefit your child as they mature.

It's astonishing to consider that if a person sets aside just $20 a month when their child is born, that when that child reaches the age of eighteen-years-old, there will be over $4000 waiting for the child and that doesn't include interest. Considering that, if a parent saves $100 or $200 a month the savings naturally accumulate faster.

Teaching the child to save is also essential to their future success. You can sit down with a child as young as eight or ten-years-old and set a family budget plan for them. Explain to them that each week when you give them an allowance you will also be depositing an equal amount in a savings account for them. Liken it to their piggy bank. They'll feel proud knowing that their hard work, whether it's brushing the dog's coat or cleaning their room is helping to set up their future.

Whenever you set a family budget consider the benefits of investing in your child's future. A firm foundation of financial understanding is priceless for a child. They feel the importance of saving and will strive to contribute to their own future as well. It's a wonderful way for any parent to teach the basics of money to their child.

Helping A Young Person Set Up A Budget

Teenagers often decide to get a part-time job. They work after school and weekends to have some spare change in their pocket or in some cases to save for something special. For a parent who has ever set a family budget, they recognize the value in guiding a child to do the same.

Sometimes when a young person has their first taste of financial freedom that comes with a part-time job, they purchase things they don't really need. They see the money as a never ending source of video games or snack foods. For a parent watching the child spending their hard earned money, it can be a bitter financial pill to swallow. There are steps that you as a parent can take to help your child see the value in saving some of that money for a bigger and brighter reward.

When a teenager gets their first job, it's time for their parent or parents to sit down and have a talk about money. If the child has grown up in an environment where the parents where frugal and explained the process of saving to the child, he or she will likely already have a desire to save. They've witnessed, first hand, the importance of saving and the rewards that can come from that.

The same can be said for children who have been involved when the parents have set a family budget. They've seen how much things like groceries or entertainment items cost and they realize that by saving they have the security of having available funds when they need them.

Offer your child guidance as they step out into the work world. By helping them set up a budget for themselves, you will give them the fundamental financial tools they will use for the rest of their lives.

Starting Young: Teaching Teens To Save Money

Teens essentially receive their parent's participation in their finances and hence it is not very wise to state that they pay no attention to parents. An issue with money is usually delicate especially when it is concerning teens.

The current trend

Part-time summer jobs have helped teenagers to earn quite a lot in the recent years. Although it is true that most often teenagers exhaust all that they earn, it is also not untrue that few of them consider savings. Be it for college education or a bigger purchase, a number of teenagers did manifest some savings Families impact a lot on the way a teenager blows up money. Teens are exceedingly responsive when it comes to their family lifestyle and source of income. Keeping the family financial status in mind, they apply similar ideology as they venture undertakings on their own.

Consequently, it lands up on parents as an accountability to guide their teenager with money matters.

Being a parent, there are ways you can help your teenage kid to set-aside the well-merited means in forms of savings or investments.

Mend your style

Teenagers tend to copy your routine most often. They would check the way you spend money and maintain the essence. For an instance, if teenagers find their parents setting aside money for some explicit household expense, then it is mostly seen that they do the identical activity when they are autonomous with money.

Assist in opening a Bank account

Instituting a bank account for your teenager under the primary name would instantaneously give the fundamental financial responsibility to him. You can then co ordinate with him or her to explain the way a bank account works, the rewards concerning savings and associated things with the same.

Furthermore, they would always have a sense of triumph when there is enough savings which could go towards their further education or procurement of some tangible asset. You may also suggest them in case of bank benefits existing for any early-age savings account.

Rise up the Spending Graph

Teenagers detest the sound of "budget" as it gives them a sense of confinement to their own possessions. In view of this, it is implied to help your daughter or son by developing a simple spending plan. This would help them key-up and imagine the ways they can spend and also minimize on things which are not of immediate necessity.

You can also have them note down their expenses and gains so that they know where they go with the unwanted spending. This would assist them to distinguish and choose between their immediate needs and luxury "wants" so that they decide on those items they can rule out to have!

The dummy stock market

As a parent you can let them be sensitive of the financial options available. You can offhandedly get them to the business section of the daily newspaper and show them about the stocks of companies. Subsequently, you can encourage them to make dummy investments for their favorite manufacturing companies. Scrutinizing these stocks in concert would let them know about the value added options when investments are spoken about.

Teens, though reluctant to ask, always wish their parents giving them inputs on monetary aspects.

The above ways would no doubt get the most of your kid's richly-deserved means.

Teach Your Children Budget Saving Tricks

To set a family budget takes more than a calculator and a list of expenses. To successfully plan and save a family has to find ways to not only save but make money. Most families have a steady stream of income and in those cases their main objective will be to save enough to afford them things like a yearly vacation and a new car every once in a while.

Each family has **money saving tips** they use when they set a family budget. Here's a few that you might not have thought of:

Lower the heat when you leave in the morning. It's costly to heat a home and doing so all day when everyone is at school or work is not needed. Turn the heat down a few degrees as you exit the house and the first person who comes in at the end of the day is responsible for turning it back up.

Have a rule regarding lights. Teaching children when they are young to turn off lights as they leave a room is a great habit to form. It saves electricity costs which can be substantial.

Plant a garden in the spring. This is not only a great method of saving on food costs it's also fun for children to help in the planting and growing. The food will taste even better to them knowing they had a hand in nurturing it.

If you had a goal of making more money when you set a family budget, **here are a few tips that may help you:**

Gather together any and all things in your home you no longer use and host a garage or yard sale. Children can join in by selling toys they no longer play with.

Take up a newspaper route with your child. This is a wonderful first job for children and it also gives them the benefit of exercise. For the parent tagging along, the work-out is not only making them a wee bit richer; it's also a great way to spend time with your children.

With a few adjustments any family can set a family budget that works for them. It's an ongoing process and with hard work the payouts can benefit each and every member of the family.

Money Saving Tips: Keep Your Social Life Intact

When young professionals practice the two week tally of expenses, they are usually shocked to find how much of their earnings go to entertainment. The cost of eating out at restaurants and bars can add up quite quickly. One does not have to eat out at fancy 5 star restaurants to quickly be down 100 dollars. The average price of a meal can set you back a few days pay. When you consider that young professionals eat out 2-3 times per weeks one can see how quickly many of them end up in debt.

There are ways to have a good social life and save money. You will definitely have to cut down on meals and nights out but you will not have to cut down on fun. Consider having friends over for dinner and drinks instead of going out. This provides for a lovely social atmosphere at a fraction of the cost.

If you take 50 dollars as the average cost for a dinner for 2 at a restaurant, you can take that same 50 dollars and cook a great meal for 5 or 6 people. Your friends will enjoy being cooked for and your home provides quite a good social atmosphere. You will also have the added advantage of being in your own home and not have to endure noise and crowds from the outside.

Having friends over for dinner and drinks is a great way to cut back the costs and still have a social life. If you socialize with the same group of people, suggest taking turns. By doing this all of you will save on entertainment and enjoy some excellent times together.

Money Saving Tips: Getting Through the Day

If you think your quite fiscally responsible and never waste money, ask yourself the following questions. How often to you buy a quick coffee at a specialist chain? How often to you purchase lunch at work or even go out? How often to you buy snacks or newspapers during your working day? Chances are you do one or more of these things on a daily basis. Spending 4-5 dollars on a coffee doesn't seem like much but these can add up. The same holds true for lunches and treats like snacks, newspapers and magazines.

IF you did each of these everyday soon you would only be working to support the purchase of these items. There are alternatives it just takes a little creativity. Buying specialist coffee can result in an expenditure annually of 1000-1600 dollars. If the thought of giving up your morning coffee sends your heart racing, the good news is you don't have to. You can save nearly 90% of this amount by brewing your own and taking it with you. Some even save the paper cups from the shops and put the coffee in those. You won't notice the difference in taste but you will notice the difference in cost.

By purchasing lunches at work, you could be spending close to 1200 dollars a year. Again, nearly 90% of this money could be saved by preparing lunches and taking them with you. You also have the added benefit of having what you choose.

Newspapers are another thing that we can completely eliminate. Chances are we read only a few sections and discard the rest. You could try getting up early and watching about 30 minutes of the morning news. This will give you all of the headlines and it is free. If you simply must have that newspaper in your hand then look for places that give them away for free. There are more than you think and are quite good.

It is okay to treat ourselves to these things once in a while but purchasing them daily results in lots of money being wasted.

Money Saving Tips: Shopping

Sooner or later we all have to hit the stores. We either have to buy food or new clothing. Believe it or not it is possible to do both of these things on quite a small budget. You don't have spent your entire salary on one simple shopping trip.

The first rule of thumb is, leave the plastic at home. Take your credit and debit cards out of your wallet and get used to using cash. When you spend actual cash, an entirely different message gets sent to your brain. You suddenly see the real cost of things. We have become so dependent on credit and debit cards that spending 5 dollars feels the same as 5 thousand.

If you are shopping for food, look for the store brand labels. Most major grocery stores have them and they are generally much cheaper than the major brands. You don't have to worry about the quality because it is the same stuff.

Of you like going out in the evenings, try doing some grocery shopping then. Many stores start to mark down their perishable items at this time. This is a great way to pick up a few things for substantial savings. As long as you use the items quite quickly they should be fine.

By practicing a few tips you can shave hundreds of off your grocery bill. Look for store brands and shop a little later. You'll be amazed at what you can save.

Money Saving Tips: Buying Clothes

We all want to look nice and clothes are a great way to do it. There is also nothing like a spot of retail therapy to cheer you up after a rotten day at work. The down side to all of this is that clothes can be quite expensive. A new outfit can set you back several hundred dollars. The good news is there are ways around this.

You can save a fortune by hitting the sales. Fashion runs 6 months ahead of schedule so as soon as summer arrives; the stores are clearing out their summer stock to make room for the fall and winter. This is a great time to pick up some great bargains. It isn't uncommon to see savings of 70-80 percent at an end of season sale. You can get some gorgeous clothing and time to enjoy it.

When you go into smaller shops, look for the sales racks. Nearly all stores have them and again, you can pick up some great things. Many times items you like will be marked down 70-80 percent. It isn't hard to spot a bargain if you have patience and time.

Finally, don't be afraid to shop at outlet malls. Many of the major clothing chains have outlet stores. Much of their stock gets sent there. They clothes are the same as you would find in the local chains but are marked down quite significantly. By making a trip to an outlet mall you could save about 50 percent on the same clothes you would by in your local shopping mall.

Contrary to popular belief, it is possible to save money in today's world. By being patient and putting some thought into the things that you buy, you will find you're enjoying life as well as saving cash.

Saving Money And Your Bills: Tips On How To Be Money Wise

Just like anyone else, I too found it quite irresistible going to the supermarket until some time back. It was one thing that always gave me a push forward, till the time I realized that this is one of the major things burning holes in my pockets. Now that I am conscious about this fact, I have made sure to stick to simple rules. Grocery shopping, for an instance, is now implied just once. With the innumerable bills to pay off, knowing the art of savings seems to be the only option.

You are not rich by considering how much you earn. It is rather bearing in mind, how much you save. This could ascertain the ease of jolly prospects ahead. For this to become true, it is essential to save on your regular monthly bills.

You can develop a checklist to know if you are making efforts to cost-cut your bills. Checking the few elementary pointers below would definitely be of assistance.

Was it the bill that gave you the electric shock?

No wonder, electricity bills take away a majority of what otherwise could have been your savings. You can definitely make sure; you get the best with your power supply. Electricity is for your comfort, hence; don't let its bill turn you down. Make it certain that you turn off those appliances which are not in use. It is as simple as that!

Energy saving lights towards practical savings... Yes, it is possible!

There are innumerable options today, so that you don't run on huge Power-bills. The power-saving lamps such as fluorescent lamps assure less consumption of power providing with ample illumination.

Water could leak your savings too; beware!

Not many take in the fact that a small leakage in any of the pipes could add to your water-bill. Water is not just precious and should not be wasted, but also when you fritter it away, you do it at your own cost!

Being tech-savvy cuts your phone bills

It has been seen that people who don't rely much on Emails and Chat servers tend to double their phone bills than those who do! Internet ensures that you can contact long distances at no huge expense like the phone.

Insulating home is insulating your pocket

Right insulation at home specifically turns down your expenses on electricity. Seldom do people recognize the amount of power that gets frittered due to bad and no insulation.

Saving money is all up to us. Reducing those sky-high bills would help us fill in some savings for unknown upcoming prospects. Being shrewd and cutting redundant expenses is equivalent to taking the first step.

You Can Rely On Banks; They Do Work!

People flock towards banking...

The subject matter of financial management would direct even corporate experts to reach an accord implying banks are the most effective, reliable and secure means to manage money. Be it bill payments, tracking transactions or obtaining earnings, banks would undeniably act as good chums besides helping you keep your savings lucrative.

Assisting in saving efficiently is undoubtedly the most apparent feature of any bank, however conceivably, not many consider this benefit. Being a fiscal conciliator, there are various means by which banks help in efficient savings.

First step towards savings; maintaining specified minimal balance

No matter what amount you withdraw from your account, the bank entails a minimal balance for continuing your partnership with them. This policy simply interprets a mandatory savings from your end.

Account is idle? You are still benefiting!

Whether or not you append to your already existing account, you enjoy the ad infinitum interest on your money.

Savings interest rates are obvious as they are paid in lieu of leaving your savings with the bank. This money is utilized by the bank for various loan disbursals through which the bank again earns interest from its customers. Effectively, this income through interest in turn oozes to you in form of savings interest rates.

Well, you might wonder, how can this be a valuable incentive system? It is a real spur, as you get more returns on your savings when your deposit with the bank is higher, comparatively.

Looking for added interest rates...? It is possible!

Banks have alternative long-term deposit plans which could be availed keeping certain threshold sum with them.

This would assist better and higher yields. These plans could be Time-deposit accounts, mutual funds or similar plans, wherein the bank would expect the monetary possessions to be unscathed for a little longer. To substitute for this obligatory time clause, banks offer you higher interest rates which in percentage are most often twice as much as that of regular savings account. Toppings to increase your capital are welcomed even in such accounts making you evidently get superior interest gains.

Money: it does grow!

Conversing with your nearest bank would help you become proficient about the available schemes that they offer. Banks propose assorted means for availing consumers to rely on them with regards to their funds. Nonetheless, in a bank you can be assured of your monetary growth besides it being a safer place for your liquid funds.

Take Charge Of Your Finances: Tips On Budgeting

So you think you need budgeting?

Prices you saw in the yesteryears are of very low magnitude for the current year. Rising internal inflation has made people to believe that a tactful plan is required for getting the greatest value for money. Money needs to be well-spent so that it maximizes your monetary funds.

You need to diplomatically work out to coordinate your earnings and expenditure so that you get the hold of being financially stable as a corporate entity.

What determines your budgeting?

Your earnings, way of life, expenditure habits, job profile and house site tells you how you can establish your level of budgeting. As you learn to maintain your expenses professionally, would be at your foremost sense of self-fulfillment.

Following below are some of the pointers which would assist you to administer your savings giving the latest outlook.

1) **Treat Math as your Lifetime Partner**- Always be smart by keeping in mind the prices of items which are regularly bought as few stores follow premature price changes on goods. It is a worthwhile decision to weigh the prices against several stores before you end up finalizing one. Limiting to a single place, whatsoever the reason is never a good idea.

Using Chinese techniques of buying in larger quantities could also add to the worth.

2. 2) **Never gamble**- Gambling would frenzy your life in a mess. It would strip you off your funds making you vulnerable to economic failures

2. 3) **Classify the wants and needs**- Shopping would become a nuisance when you are not aware of how to prioritize the requirements. The fundamentals of food, clothing and shelter cannot be done without. These requirements are worth throwing spend at, as they concern your health and security coming under the needs category. Wants can always wait as they are associated with luxury which can be done without.

4. 4) **Don't spend exceeding what you earn**- It is not what you earn that makes you rich, but it is what you save! At times the idiom "Rags to Riches" become vice versa. Be diplomatic with your shopping expenditure and you would be amazed to visualize your wise spending.

4. 5) **Maintain the basic list**- It is advisable to agree on things that are key and imperative to you. It is good to conclude what item is required and which are the ones you only long to have.

The foremost thing that people don't realize is the significance of buying according to one's lifestyle. Keeping your style at the base, you can decide what is really necessary. Unless you are a frivolous customer who is abundant of resources, you have no choice but to accept the above.

Self-Control And Saving Money

Does self-control really work?

Although, everybody has Self-control imbibed within them, most often people don't implement it diplomatically resulting in unexpected spending sprees. Knowing self-control right would make considerable difference in the way people handle money. Self-control makes sure that you go more towards the savings end rather than on frivolous expenditure. Most of all, you can be relieved of the urge to spend unwittingly as people always do as soon as they get the grip of money.

Beware of the common mistake

This is the most widespread downside most people face. Habitually, it so happens that you tend to sprint on shopping sprees when you think a good amount is accumulated. Majority of them have such overwhelming push to satisfy their urge. This could turn out to be perilous. Whenever you find such urge trying to get the best out of your lack of self-control, you must measure the sketch of your future. A thought of your future should immediately narrow your unwanted expenses.

Nothing is really constant

It is evidently true that nothing is really constant. Whatever looks glossy and new-fangled would no doubt fade away in a while. Your command over self control would make you appreciate many other imperative things which oblige more of your concern when spending is thought about!

Financial triumph on basis of self control

Any financial victory begins with the effort of reducing and taking care of fancy expenses.

How do acquire the art of controlling expenses?

Self control is no doubt indefinable. Most often people avoid things which could be easily implemented. There are a few ways which are even less dense to approach towards self control. If you follow these little steps from the stepladder, they will bear brilliant fruits making you financially sturdy and defensive. It is implied that you become skilled with self-control and develop yourself with its breed.

Never purchase items when you get the terrific impulse towards it. If you re-consider your thinking, you would know if it is really required or can wait, benefiting from that extravagant expenditure.

Classify to know what are your needs and wants. It should never happen that the result of your action today, causes you regrets in future.

Keep a person to be your role-model so that you can also familiarize yourself with his economic lifestyle. This would help you a lot as when you see others following a self controlled life style, you are most likely to find your feet too, in it!

Money Savings On Food

Coffee Drinker! Are you one?

It is quite passable to re-use the grounded coffee just once. Carrying this on for about three times too, would not impinge on the coffee flavor. Executing this idea is vastly encouraged, provided you use a more permanent filter, shunning the paper variety. In case of multiple re-uses, the coffee grounds could be refrigerated till it is used on the subsequent day.

So you are the typical Bread Lover!

Bread is no doubt essential. It is often found that grocery stores vend bread at a considerably lower price when they are a day old. It is found to be nothing off beam eating day old bread especially when it is equally good consume. You can stockpile it for bigger savings when there is ample scope within the refrigerator. Frozen bread could always be defrosted using the microwave oven; however it should be ensured that it is reheated every thirty seconds so that the bread-ends remain soft.

Buying from the grocery? Keep in mind...

There are a few things to be taken care before purchasing grocery. Most of all, it is required to list the things that are really indispensable. Giving the top priority to basic goods would help in staying away from things that are junk. It is suggestive to keep an eye on price displays always remembering that branded harvests are unquestionably expensive compared to store trademarks. One can always keep the receipts of grocery store visits, so that it makes your next visit on priority too! To encompass better savings, products could be bought on bulk which could then be hoarded either in the refrigerator or at the peace of your shelves. This notion is tricky enough to minimize your strolls to the provision store.

Whilst you Visit or devour outside....

So your plan is to go to some high-priced bistro? Then the finest occasion would be all through the lunch hour. Lunches are always at reduced rates complementing the pro. When planning for trips comprising hotel stays, it is always good to be well-turned-out and uncover to check if the hotel incorporates breakfast in the total room charge. You should also make an effort to check the food-joints where the locals go. They would apparently know places where better quality food is dished up for a much reasonable price. While going around, carrying snacks such as a chocolate bar, chips or cookies would come a longer way in the run.

Being calculative in buying and planning for food-entries does not essentially mean consuming awful rations. It only says that you are looking at the many alternatives available around you, of which you can widely choose from. There is no dearth of options available in the Food-industry. Making smart choices without being dicey would not just get you towards good edibles, but also help you decently reduce your superfluous outlay.

Save Money And Save The World

If you vision a great future for yourself and your loved-ones then all you need to learn is the fixture to your monetary savings. Your savings could either yield you tangible assets what you always longed for be it a dream home or a new car. Or it could be a way towards your child's college education or even better, a cruise towards the South African Safari!

There are untold ways you can go about your savings. For an instance, it could be keeping aside some bit from your regular income or staying away from fancy urges which often arise of nowhere!

1. Combined effort at home

It is implied that savings in a family should become a joint effort. Family future prospects require all members to be a part of it.

2. Take care about the fuel

Driving short distances when, as a matter of fact, these drives could be avoided, is never a good idea. Nearby places could always be taken by foot. Substituting your bike for the car is again advisable. When you know that there are many people en route to your workplace, pooling car would always be a great notion.

3. Those petty urges!

Start making it a habit to pass up those little tempting appeals coming your way. Fulfilling yourself once in a while would be a good idea, however overdoing it needs to be restricted.

4. Reducing the extravaganza

Electricity: No wonder, electricity bills take away a majority of what otherwise could have been your savings. You can definitely make sure; you get the best with your power supply. Electricity is for your comfort, hence; don't let its bill turn you down. Make it certain that you turn off those appliances which are not in use. It is as simple as that! The power-saving lamps such as fluorescent lamps assure less consumption of power providing with ample illumination.

5. Water

Not many take in the fact that a small leakage in any of the pipes could add to your water-bill. Going for luxury showers always could be avoided. Water is not just precious and should not be wasted, but also when you fritter it away, you do it at your own cost!

6. Phone

It has been seen that people who don't rely much on Emails and Chat servers tend to double their phone bills than those who do! Internet ensures that you can contact long distances at no huge expense like the phone.

7. Gas

If you are planning to go for a new automobile purchase, make sure you check its fuel efficiency. Enjoying the cool breeze would be a better alternative than keeping the Air conditioning on every time.

People fail to recognize that savings become decent only when miniscule household utilities don't go redundant. The benefits are like 2 faces of the coin; you get that longing extra cent, plus, you contribute towards energy savings.

Tips On How To Save Money When Shopping

People have unexplainable addiction towards shopping. They are most often ready to let go the household budget when shopping is on the curve. Shopping would become a nuisance only when you are not aware of how to plan your expenses right! Just a few things to be kept in mind and there you go....

Estimate and take the precise amount of money!

A wise shopper would always make that educated guess to know how much it would cost him for the entire shopping. It is always implied that you don't carry more cash than whatever is estimated. Estimation could be done by making a list of requisites and prioritizing the most important things. This would be the foremost step which would assist in reduction of frivolous shopping.

Think twice to judge the right price

It is a worthwhile decision to weigh the prices against several stores before you end up finalizing one. Limiting to a single place, whatsoever the reason is never a good idea. Quite a few stores provide you with a value-for-money deals ensuring quality intact. One can always be smart by keeping in mind the prices of items which are regularly bought as few stores follow premature price changes on goods.

Why not shop for summers in the spring?

Season ending sale does not always compromise on the worth of goods. The prices for woolens are usually affordable during the threshold of summers. Likewise, spring is great time to shop for Summer-wear.

Something worthy to suit your budget!

Places like Dollar-shops too, uncover moderately priced items which are perhaps on sale at times. While the eminence of few goods here cannot be compared to those in malls and shopping galleries, the merchandises are innovative and never worn-out. Why not try them to see as they offer preeminent prices to survive with!

Optimizing the conveyance effort

Ever wondered why we shop for too long? Most often we end up travelling in search of stores for our requisites and never realize that this again appends to our shopping expense. It is also recommended that you verify the prices of regularly bought items on your daily en route, if they are in any budgeted price range. Buying in these circumstances would help you save fuel and time even though it is early for your shopping agenda!

Discounts really count!

Undertaking to check concession stores which never compromise on quality would yield a lot. Most of these stores have discounts based on times of the year. You can locate such stores in outsized shopping areas like malls and shopping galleries.

With shopping guidelines at your bay why not review your idea of dreadful-shopping and make shopping a congenial and delightful experience?

Secrets Of Keeping To The Family Budget

Being wise is next to simple

Inflation conversely means having reasonable amount of savings for the future unknown, from the skimpy income you get. This however doesn't mean anything dreary as long as you are budgeting right and know about prioritizing alternatives.

Tribulations in finance usually occur due lack of accurate budgeting skills or negligence in sticking to the projected plan. Regardless of what your income is, it is essential to maintain notes of your assets and liabilities along with gains and expenditures.

Though it sounds paradoxical, anyone whose income is in thousands has plights similar to another who is earning lesser. Habitually, people no matter what their earning-levels are, have continuous budgeting problems. Quite a few of them, in spite of having a pre-planned budget find it tricky to stick to it.

So what exactly is budgeting?

A budget is more of a fiscal plan, which takes into account, the incoming and outgoing monetary funds. Budgeting involves spending less on whimsical things resulting from bottom priority so that the savings get ample stipend.

This would assist in maintaining moderate equilibrium between earnings and expenditure.

How does budgeting start?

First of all it is assumed that all budgeting is done once the tax liabilities are settled. Next, regardless of what you earn, you need to figure out the primary expenses, be it concerning food, transportation or house-related.

This then needs to be deducted from the total earnings after tax to see what is left out. This residue is termed to be a saving!

Savings have an advantage at a later point in time and that would be when the real need comes up.

No matter where you keep the savings amount, though preferably bank, you must ensure that this is free form not just intruders but you yourself! If you think you have got that added lump of thick savings then a financial advisor could be helpful in managing your portfolio.

Follow the pointers to remain within your family budget...

Listing income and expenditure daily, weekly or at any schedule would help you visualize about funds wisely

Grocery shopping is implied just once. You can decide a marked period for getting the groceries and make a listing of all the things required before the target date. You may perhaps get discounts on buying at bulk in most stores.

Don't decide to step into a supermarket unless you really have a primary requisite. Most of them don't stick to this and end up spending on junk, drifting away from the budget.

Thinking wisely, and twice, before any purchase would always make you comprehend that most of the things are mere luxury wants and whims and can wait for a better time.

High-Low Numbers: Tips On Saving Money On Clothes

You will have to determine exactly what you want when it comes to picking the clothes to wear. You may choose to get the best dresses, bags and shoes in town, but more importantly, you should consider the prices first.

It is always necessary when choosing the clothes to buy to identify your taste as to ascertaining whether to go for the best designer clothing or just about anyone you see.

The way you are dressed determines how you are addressed. People relate to you based on the way you dress. It is vital to point out here that you can dress very well, looking attractive with just little money. A good fashion taste does not mean it must be very expensive. You can look very fashionable without having to spend so much.

If you want to make a mark with your dress sense without spending so much, I will advise you go through the following **steps to ensure that money is saved** while still looking your best.

1. 1. The first step is to calculate properly before shopping for clothes. After your calculation, shop for the best in relation to the amount of money available. Instead of buying one very expensive outfit, you can get several outfits with that exact amount of money, without altering your beautiful sense of fashion - You will still look good with the less expensive clothes and save more money too.

1. 2. Do not go shopping for clothes without first establishing the exact type and design you want. Get your needs and window shop, evaluating the different prices available at different stores. With this, you will know exactly where to get what you need at the

cheapest price - hence saving money on your clothes.

1.   3.   One of the best ways to save money on your clothes is to do your shopping at the thrift shop. The clothes sold at these shops are very affordable since they are donations made to charity. These shops are nonprofit organizations giving all its proceeds to the less privileged ones in the society.

Because of the reason, the thrift shop is a better choice when shopping for clothes because it is cost effective, helping you to save money instead of wasting it on expensive wears. And, you can use this medium to also donate money to the less privileged.

Whenever you want to shop for clothes, go for the very durable ones, even if they are cheap, because durable clothes last longer, and this will help you to save money.

The Advantages Of Using Money Budgeting Software

There are a lot of people in debt today because of the act of expending more than the income. Some are now addicted to credit cards that their monthly earnings are just spent on debt repayment - Is there a way out of this?

Yes, there is a way out of this cycle of debt. One can only get a relief from debts when he or she embraces the act of financial planning called budgeting. In this system, every expense is carefully analyzed before execution; the monthly income is planned seriously, leading to careful and not careless expenditures.

Some people lack the skill of logically and analytically planning their finances and this hinders their efforts to live a financially free life; hence a need for financial planning software is necessitated.

This is the origin of the planning software to enhance the analogy and calculation of your expanses providing the way out of any debt situation. This software is called the budgeting software.

The financial planning software assists the user to plan his or her monthly income properly by allocating funds to the different areas of need, giving priority to the most important; there is also an amount kept aside on a monthly basis for saving.

The planning software is needed by all for financial budgeting because of the **following reasons**:

1. With the financial planning or budgeting software one can keep a tab on the amount of money spent each month, because the software helps the user to monitor his or her monthly expenses. It will show you where all your money goes.

2. The financial planning software will also assist the user to make futuristic goals. This is an edge the software has over the physical method of writing your plans on paper.

It lets you see into the financial future, providing the opportunity to plan ahead to meet needs in the future.

3. The money planning software helps to manage the way money is spent monthly, keeping a watch on your monthly expenditures. With this software, you will no longer spend money on impulse; every dollar spent will be a result of careful calculation.

This will help you control the amount of money you spend every month and also keep you out of debt, since unnecessary expenditures are cut off and purchases are restricted to using the cash at hand, instead of borrowing to unavailable to get the available.

Finally, you should never spend money without planning, do away with the attitude of impulsive spending, every purchase should be calculative analyzed before proceeding with it. That you are sure of managing your finances well and having an excess in the account for futuristic purposes.

Tips On Saving Money During The Holidays

There is always excitement in the air during festive seasons like Thanksgiving Day, Christmas and New Year celebrations. In these special seasons there are exchanges of gifts from person to person and from family to family; all these calls for a lot of shopping.

If care is not taken in times like these, one will end up spending excessively on irrelevant things.

It is important to buy gifts during holidays, yes! But, how much do you spend? You can easily buy a lovely gift to appreciate someone without the need to spend so much on it. There is a need to economies your financial resources during festive seasons, so as to have more money in the future.

1. The first step towards economizing your financial resources is to have a financial spending plan for the festive season.

After setting up this financial spending plan, Endeavour to follow it, adhering strictly to the underlying details. This means that the step by step plan should be followed during the holiday season, so as to avoid excess spending.

2. Bear in mind that you can only give out what you have, when buying gifts during the festive seasons be constrained by the limits of your purse, do not spend above your present resources and avoid the use of credit cards.

It is not wise to incur so much debt in festive seasons that you might spend the rest of the New Year repaying. Operate within the boundaries of your income.

3.   3.   It is better to send specially made casual gifts: you can create one yourself, just by being imaginative and creative. These ones have more effects and are cheaper to get. The gifts with a personal touch are more

appreciated than others; this is an easy way out.

3.   4.   Finally, before buying anything during the festive periods, be sure to go around different shops to get the prices of the item to be purchased, after doing this, you can now evaluate the difference in the prices to see the most suitable price before buying.

It is always good to window shop, this act allows you to search and evaluate the differences in prices and quality; at the end, and the best choice is made with the most affordable price. Do not be in the habit of sticking to only one shop; it is not the best thing to do.

The Festive Seasons are surely the best time in the year, but don't be carried away by the excitement and fun of the holiday; you have to be logical and strategic in your shopping.

Enjoy the holiday and make sure you economize your financial resources.

A Family Budget For Every Day And Not Just The Rainy Days

One of the aspects of family life that people rarely enjoy dealing with is to set a family budget. It can be an arduous task filled with disagreement. One family member might see entertainment as a fundamental part of the budget, while another views it as a luxury that isn't needed. Finding a common middle ground and sticking to it will guarantee financial success.

A budget is essentially a summary of lists of intended expenses and expected incomes. The aim is to strike a balance between income and expenses. Setting up a family budget can be different from one family to another based on their specific needs. While one family might feel content to save a certain percentage of their income to buy a car another would be satisfied with the idea of keeping their older vehicle and dedicating those funds to an annual family vacation. And not all family budgets are set in place by the family while sitting at their kitchen table. Some family budgets are designed by experienced financial planners and agents. But the intention is always the same, planning for present expenses and also preparing for the unexpected.

When you set out to set a family budget it's imperative that you consider all of the financial needs and goals of each individual and also the family as a collective whole. Therefore it's important to include the cost of items such as:

Children's college funds.

Saving for a new home or home improvements.

Retirement savings.

Saving for the unforeseeable, such as car repairs or loss of employment.

Every conceivable expense needs to be calculated as you work through the process to set a family budget.

Naturally the adults will have the last say as they are generally the ones contributing the income to the running and maintenance of the household. Children's needs have to be addressed as well, including the possibility of having to purchase items such as prescription eyeglasses or braces. If you don't have a medical insurance plan to help supplement the cost of these items, they can take a fairly good bite out of your budget.

There are professional financial planners who are highly experienced in working with people to set a family budget. They generally do charge for their services and if you are trying to save money they can be viewed as either an investment or perhaps just an expense if you feel you can handle the process on your own. Another alternative might be to research any workshops in your area that are designed to help when it comes time to set a family budget. These can be either low-cost or no-cost and the information is extremely valuable.

Going through the motions to set a family budget can save you a substantial amount of money over time. No one likes to fall short in the financial department and not be able to provide for their family.

With a reasonable budget in place, money worries can be a thing of the past, it just takes some planning and dedication.

Set A Family Budget With Professional Assistance

If you've tried in vain to set a family budget and it's constantly failing, it might be time to turn to a professional for help. Many people struggle with spending and saving and often find that they are unable to make ends meet. If that is the case, it's priceless having the guidance of someone who has a strong understanding of money matters.

Seeking out the services of a professional budget planner is a step in the right direction if budgeting isn't your strong suit.

It might seem embarrassing to seek out the help of a stranger to set a family budget. After all, money is a private matter, and if you can't handle the juggling act of paying your bills and providing for your family, won't a budget planner view you as a financial failure? They won't.

Budget planners are experienced in helping people in all income brackets develop a plan to manage their resources and at the same time keep their heads above the financial waters. They can work closely with you to help you not only pay your bills but budget for a savings account as well.

The first step when you visit a professional to help you set a family budget is to be completely honest with them. Bring along copies of your pay stubs and also be ready and willing to reveal what you are spending money on and how much money it is. In order for a budget planner to really give you the best service they can, they need to know exactly what they have to work with.

Any documentation you have in relation to household expenses will be helpful to them. Armed with that and with the insight they will have garnered from interviewing you they will be able to set a family budget plan that will help you reach your financial goals.

The budget planner will explain the situation to you and your family. They will outline exactly what steps you need to reach your financial goals. Often this means significant changes in spending habits. You may have grown accustomed to shopping for new clothes once a month and the budget planner may insist that in order to set a family budget plan that addresses all of your financial needs that your clothes shopping adventures have to be curtailed to once a year with a set amount of money allocated to that.

It's important to listen and absorb what the budget planner is telling you. Their objective is to make your life easier by relieving you of the ongoing burden you've felt when it comes to money matters. Their suggestions and ideas are designed specifically for your family and the individual needs that you have.

Working with a professional to set a family budget plan isn't always easy. But the effort and frustration you felt will quickly turn to gratification when you realize that by adopting and embracing their suggestions, your money situation looks a lot brighter.

Set a Family Budget Easily By Tracking Expenses

Small expenses can equal a big chunk of a families' budget. When you spend a few dollars at the movie theater or have dinner out once or twice a week, those seemingly minor expenses can quickly accumulate into a lot of money. Often, we don't realize how much until we actually write it down.

A great first step when you get ready to set a family budget is to journal your daily expenses. This can feel like a time consuming and tedious task but the benefits far outweigh any frustration.

All you need to do is purchase a small note pad that you can keep either in your handbag or your pocket along with a pen. Whenever you purchase anything, you jot it down on the note pad. It doesn't matter if it's something as insignificant as a package of chewing gum or a bottle of water. You must mark down the item, the time of day you purchased it and the price. Do this all day, including everything you spend money on.

When it's time to sit down and set a family budget, each family member can present their note pads. This way all money being spent can be accounted for. Doing this enables the person who is responsible for the budget to get a clearer view of what money is being spent on. Making an effort to journal expenses also provides the family an opportunity to review their expenses and determine what non-essentials are soaking up resources.

One area where many families spend a great deal of money without realizing it is on convenience or fast foods. Stopping at a corner store to purchase a sandwich each day can add up to a substantial amount of money over a month.

The same can be said for items such as soda or juice from a vending machine. On average, these items cost several times more when coming from a vending machine, than they do if they are purchased at a grocery store in the form of a dozen or two dozen carton. If you add those savings up over the period of a month and multiply that amount by four family members, that's a nice sum of money.

Taking a few days to keep track of daily expenses is invaluable information when it comes time to set a family budget. It puts a spotlight on unnecessary expenses. Armed with this arsenal of information any family can find ways to save money. For instance, if your child is purchasing a candy bar on their way home from school each day, buy them in bulk and keep them handy so they can grab one before they leave for the day. The same can be said with bottled water. Buying a case cuts the cost per bottle substantially and if you stock them in the refrigerator, they made for a cool and cheap treat.

Investing a few minutes to write down what you've purchased can save a good deal of money each year. It's a task that every family member can take part in and also reap the financial rewards from.

Set A Family Budget With Food Costs In Mind

Ask any family what a significant fraction of their monthly income goes to and they will say its food. We all need to eat and most people also want to keep their families healthy by purchasing and preparing meals that are good for them.

For a growing family of four this can be a challenge. Food is not inexpensive and if you're feeding children it can seem as though they are always eating. When it comes time to set a family budget, you have to consider not only what you are eating, but what it is costing you.

One factor that many people don't calculate into their food buying budget is the price of eating out. They may view this as separate from their weekly grocery bill, but the cost can be significant and should be considered.

If you are eating away from home more than twice a month, you might be doing the food portion of your family budget a disservice. Eating meals out, whether they are from a fast food establishment or a four star restaurant are costly. You are not only paying for the price of the food, but you are also contributing handsomely to the preparation costs along with the overhead of the restaurant.

It's lovely to have someone else cook for you and often this is the impetus for people to dine out. They are too tired from a stressful day to even consider the idea of putting on an apron and whipping up a dinner. Instead they look to the take-out menu or buy a pre-packaged dinner that costs several times what the individual ingredients would.

If your job is to set a family budget, you should not only look at ways to cost food costs but also consider who is responsible for preparing the meals.

If one person has to plan the menu, purchase the food and prepare it, that can become monotonous and can actually lead to a family spending more money on food because there is a greater temptation for that person to want to get away from the kitchen on occasion.

When you are sitting down to set a family budget include all members of the family. In addition to planning an affordable meal plan, also prepare a shopping and cooking schedule.

Perhaps everyone who is old enough to cook could take an active role, taking on the chore for one evening a week. This approach works well because everyone gets involved and the person who was normally the family's chef, now enjoy the luxury of being catered to.

With some alterations and planning your family's food costs can be decreased dramatically.

Choose menu plans that feed not only your appetites but fit into your bank account.

When you set a family budget consider the idea of eating meals that contain costly ingredients like meat less and meals that contain fresh vegetables more.

Not only will you save money but you'll also gain the benefit of a healthier body.

Set A Family Budget And Enjoy A Great Vacation

After working for months the idea of a family vacation can seem like the ideal reward. A week or two in a sunny climate in the middle of a cold and snowy winter is the icing on their yearly cake. Vacations are usually costly though and if your job is set a family budget, you'll want to get the most out of each dollar you've allocated to the vacation fund.

There are many important factors to consider if you've decided to set up a financial plan that includes money for vacations. It isn't enough to just take a percentage of each paycheck and put it in a separate bank account that you'll turn to at the end of the year. With the proper planning techniques in place when you set a family budget you'll be able to execute a trip that will be unforgettable.

One important consideration is timing. Most people want to venture out on a holiday at the same time each year. The travel industry refers to these times as peak periods and they generally fall in December, March and again during the summer months. The reason for this is because more people are tempted to take off on a trip when their children aren't in school. The travel industry knows this and prices are considerably higher during these times.

Although school work is most important, planning a trip during a non-peak time and preparing beforehand might be the most economical answer. Research is fundamental when planning any trip. There is an abundance of information on the internet that can give you an idea of the total cost you will be facing for your trip.

If you do decide to travel during a non-peak time and you have children enrolled in school, there are steps you can take to assist them with their studies. Talk to their teachers and have them assign homework for the trip. This is a wonderful method of not only keeping the children up to par in class but it gives them something to focus on during the car or airplane ride. Children can become agitated easily when expected to sit still for prolonged periods of time, but if they are engrossed in studies, the time moves along much more quickly.

Another consideration when you set a family budget that includes a vacation fund is to consider traveling to a destination that offers all-inclusive vacation packages.

This includes not only your airfare and accommodations but can also include meals and beverages. The savings with this type of vacation plan can be considerable. It also offers up the benefit of pre-planning all related costs. You'll know how much you need to save each month to reach your vacation goal.

One of the things that people often overlook when considering vacation expenses as they set a family budget is the benefit of visiting relatives. A destination that involves family members can result in a considerable savings in accommodation costs.

Most people welcome the company of relatives for a few days and if you buy them dinner or surprise them with a thank-you gift they'll invite you back time and time again.

Set A Family Budget That Lets You Give

December can be an overwhelming month when it comes to the family budget. For many people they want to be generous and choose a holiday gift that will adequately reflect their appreciation to the person receiving it. It's a lovely gesture but when the holiday bills start filling your mailbox and draining your bank account after the first of the year, you won't have any appreciation for the fact that you didn't plan your gift giving strategy more carefully.

When it's time to set a family budget, gift giving has to have a place. If it doesn't your

December buying binges could result in financial problems that last for the better part of the next year.

The first and most important step is to choose an amount of money that you can affordably spend and then sticking with it. This shouldn't be done while you are in the middle of a store filled with holiday decorations and tempting gift choices. This should be done early in the year, the earlier the better actually.

A common time of year to set a family budget is in January. For some people it becomes one of their New Year's Resolutions. Saving money and sticking to a budget. Along with weight loss, this resolution often doesn't make it into February. With a little willpower though you can not only lose weight but save money as well. Gift giving is an area that most people can save quite a bit of money in.

Here is a list of money saving tips that relate to gift giving:

Make your Christmas and birthday gift giving lists in January.

Pick an amount to spend on each person and don't defer from that.

Whenever you see something during the year that fits the person's interests and your budget, purchase it and set it aside for the appropriate occasion.

Homemade gifts such as greeting cards and fruit baskets are a lovely gesture and welcomed because the person giving took time to make something as opposed to purchasing it.

Discuss the idea of picking names for Christmas gift giving if you are a member of a large family. If each person spends a slightly larger amount of money on one person as opposed to a small amount on several people this allows you to not only give a nicer gift, but you save money as well.

Gift giving doesn't need to break your piggy bank. When you set a family budget, pick an amount for each person you need to buy gifts for and get shopping, knowing that this year you won't overextend yourself and your holidays really will be filled with joy.

 You'll have the joy of knowing that you've given what you can afford. Often others will appreciate a gift limit as well because it means less money they feel pressured into spending as well. The holidays are much more about family than gifts and with proper planning you can have both.

Set A Family Budget And Have Fun

One of the things that most people consider when they set a family budget is how much money to allocate to entertainment expenses. This may seem like a small portion of the money a family spends, but it can add up quickly.

Most people enjoy getting out to the movies, especially when it's time for the next blockbuster to hit the big screen. If you're planning on taking the whole family it can quickly add up to a costly night on the town. With new movies opening each weekend it's crucial when you set a family budget to think about how quickly you need to see that new release.

Most movies that are in the theater can be found on DVDs within a few months. If you are patient this can add up to substantial savings over the course of a year. Considering that the cost of purchasing the DVD is equal to, on average, the cost of two adult movie tickets, you can see the benefit in waiting a few months to see the film. An even bigger incentive is to think about the cost of renting that DVD. If you take that route, you'll be spending a very small amount to see the exact same feature film just a few short months earlier.

Although the cost of the movie tickets is going to take a big bite out of your monthly entertainment budget, there is another aspect to the theater experience that can prove expensive. That's the refreshment stand. For anyone who has been to a movie recently, they can attest to the fact that popcorn and peanuts face a huge mark-up when they are purchased inside the doors of a movie theater. For most theater goers though, it's an important part of the experience and one they don't want to forfeit in the name of a budget.

There are some steps you can take to enjoy a family outing to the movies within the limits you had when you set a family budget. Consider these ideas:

Go to a matinee instead of an evening showing. Matinees are less expensive and the show is identical.

Bring your own candy. Smaller size versions of the large movie theater candy bars are more than enough to satisfy your sweet tooth and your budget.

Purchase a bottle of water instead of a soda. Often the water in a theatre is much less expensive than buying a sugar filled soda or juice and it's better for your health as well.

Making a few small changes in your entertainment choices can result in big savings for the family. Make a night out at the movies a special event and the children will enjoy it more knowing that they don't get that luxury each week. Keep your eyes open for any discount or 2-for-1 coupons from your local DVD rental outlet. A big bowl of popcorn, a few cans of soda and some rented movies make for a fun family night that's easy on the budget.

Set A Family Budget That Includes Coupons

When your family sits down to set a family budget you might not be considering the value that coupons and rebates hold. Those little slips of paper you clip out of the newspaper and magazine can add up to big savings.

The practice of cutting coupons is decades old. People get their scissors ready and flip through newspaper inserts and magazines cutting out coupons that help them save money on a favored product. While most coupons offer a savings that might seem minute, when you put them altogether it can add up to tidy sum.

There is a craft to cutting and using coupons and rebate forms and with a little planning while you set up a family budget, you can easily save a sizable amount of money. Factoring in the savings that you'll garner from coupons isn't prudent during the budget planning stage. After all, you can't predict how much money you will save that month by using coupons. However, you can keep track of how much money you actually save and put that in a rainy day jar or a mad money bucket. That way, when you want a special treat or decide to take the family out to a nice dinner you'll already have the financial resources to do that without it impacting the decisions you made when you set a family budget.

There are a few important rules to follow to get the most value from coupons:

Use coupons on sale items. If you do this you are dramatically reducing the price of something that you generally purchase at regular price.

Watch for "double coupon days" at local stores. Some stores offer the consumer a chance to use their coupons at a double discount once a month. This can save a substantial amount of money even reducing the cost of certain items to almost nothing.

Trade coupons with friends, relatives or co-workers. Many people cut coupons and save them waiting for a chance to use them. If they have a coupon for a product you normally buy and vice versa, you can make a trade.

Visit websites that offer coupon discounts. There are many websites that have literally hundreds of dollars of discount coupons available.

All you do is point, click and print. Use rebate forms for sale items.

If you have a rebate form for a product, purchase it when it's on sale and be certain to ask for two copies of the receipt. Most rebate requests don't honor photocopied receipts and if you have two copies, both printed from the store's cash register, you can keep one for warranty purposes and use the other to mail-in for your rebate.

When you work to set a family budget in place, consider that coupons are akin to bonuses.

When you use one, take the money saved and use it one something special. The whole family will want to take part, just to get the reward!

Set A Family Budget That Includes Savings

When you and your family sit down to set a family budget plan, savings might come near the end of the list. Routine living expenses normally soak up a great deal of a family's resources and whatever is left over might be so miniscule that it won't seem worth saving. Regardless of the size, savings are a necessity.

No one can predict when life will take a turn for the worse. We rarely ever budget for illness, a broken car part or a furnace that is too old to keep us warm in the winter. These are rainy day expenses and as the old saying goes, sometimes when it rains it pours.

When you set a family budget you should consider savings as a high priority. One way to guarantee that you will save is to deduct a portion of your paycheck before you budget with it. In other words, you can take perhaps 5% or 10% of your paycheck and put it in a rainy day account. In that sense you are pretending the money isn't there and you can't be tempted to spend it. With the remainder of your paycheck you can set a family budget that will tend to your regular monthly expenses.

Another effective method of budgeting for savings is to take any extra money you receive during the year and place it in a rainy day account. This could include things like year-end bonuses at work, or income tax refunds. If you take those amounts and immediately put them in a bank account that is dedicated to emergencies, you won't have time to consider what else you could be buying with that money.

If resources are very tight when you set a family budget and savings are essentially impossible, it might be time to consider some cost cutting measures to free up some extra money. Here are a few ideas of things you can do everyday to save money:

Walk instead of drive. If you need to stop at a grocery store to fetch milk or bread and it's only a few blocks away, take a walk. It not only saves on fuel costs but the exercise won't hurt either.

Take a bagged lunch instead of buying lunch. Bought lunches can add up to a fair bit of money over the course of a year. If you prepare a lunch at home, you'll quickly notice the extra money you're saving.

Visit the library instead of the book store. Reading is a favorite pastime of many people, but it can become costly. Instead of purchasing each book you want to read, visit the library. The cost of a yearly membership is a very small fraction of what you'd normally spend on books over the course of twelve months.

By adopting a few small changes you can start saving money each month. It's always good to be prepared for any possible financial emergencies and having a saving plan in place when you set a family budget can help with that.

Set A Family Budget That Saves On Bank Fees

With the invention of the ATM machine, visiting the bank and seeing the bank teller has become a thing of the past. It's so much more convenient to drive up to an ATM, punch in your pin number and withdraw enough money to meet your current needs. The ATM is also a time-saving way to pay your bills. For many people it's the only way they bank.

All of that convenience does come at a price though and you may not even realize how much it's costing you. Almost every bank charges some fees for their customers to use ATMs and if in a pinch you have to get money quickly and the only ATM in the vicinity is another bank's it might cost you much more than you are willing to pay.

It's rare when you sit down to set a family budget to consider the price that your banking is costing you. You instead budget for things like food, utilities, housing payments and car costs. These are all essentials but the monthly fees your bank is charging you need to be taken into consideration as well.

Most monthly banking plans offer a set number of ATM transactions. If you go over this amount they are authorized to automatically charge a fee per transaction. If you frequent the ATM quite often, this can quickly add up to a significant expense.

A first step in determining how much your banking fees are impacting your finances is to look at your last banking statement. This will explain what fees you were charged and if any of them relate to your ATM usage. If they do you can make some easy changes that will help you keep the banking fees at a minimum and allow you to account for that amount when you set a family budget. If you approach it this way, your fees will always stay the same and you'll know what to expect to pay each month.

To keep banking fees at a minimum consider trying the following:

Keep a minimum balance in the account. Often banks will waive monthly fees if a minimum balance is kept in the account at all times.

Try to pay bills in alternate ways. Perhaps you can visit the department store where your credit card payment is sent or you can visit a kiosk at the company that supplies your electricity to pay the bill. Often companies will have payment drop-off boxes that may be on your way home from work. Paying this way can save ATM fees.

Withdraw as much cash as you'll need for the week. Instead of taking $20 out 5 times in the span of a week, withdraw $100 once a week. By doing that you've already saved four ATM transactions for the month.

This could keep you under the minimum and also not paying extra fees for usage.

It's also important to bear in mind that every family member who banks has to pay fees. This is something that you'll want to keep track of when you set a family budget that everyone needs to follow.

Money Saving Tips: Knowing Where To Begin

Today, with the country continually mounting up large amounts of debt. We are encouraged more and more to start putting money aside. Despite the economic prosperity of the recent decades, there could still come a time when you and your partner could find yourself out of work. To help offset this situation one should try to have 2-3 months reserve salary saved should this unfortunate event occur. However, do you ever wonder why, even though you and your partner seem to make good salaries, it is impossible to save any money? It seems to leave your account as quickly as it arrived. You want desperately to save money but you are finding it impossible.

Saving money isn't as impossible as you might think. The first major hurdle that people face when trying to save money is to organize their finances. Chances are, your spending much more money than your realize and chances are you are completely oblivious to it.

One excellent money saving tip is to start tracking all of your spending. You will need a small notebook and something to write with. This must accompany you everywhere and everything that you by must be recorded down to the last penny. It doesn't matter how small of a purchase it is, it must be listed.

You should aim to do this exercise for at least a 2 week period. This task can be quite painstaking but it is one of the most useful tools to help those wanting to break bad spending habits. Once your 2 week period has ended, you need to review all of your expenditures. You will quickly start to see where all of your money is going.

Many who complete this task are shocked to see how much money is spent on small items. 1 dollar on a newspaper, for example may seem quite insignificant but over the course of a year amounts to 365 dollars.

Once you see how much money is wasted on insignificant items such as these two things will likely happen. The first being, you'll be quite angry at yourself. It isn't uncommon for people to spend thousands of dollars in a year on objects such as newspapers, coffees and small treats. When confronted with this they tend to feel quite angry for allowing this to happen. The second being, you will implement a plan for change. You will quickly start to prioritize your spending and cut out many of those expenditures that you don't really need.

If you want to start putting money aside, a great money saving tip is to first start tracking your finances. This will show you where your money is going and help you implement a plan for change.

Money Saving Tips: Get It In The Bank

It is true, that by changing habits and being frugal, one can reduce their costs by quite a wide margin. However, it is also important to see the bank balance start to grow. Saving money seems to be very difficult for many people. They either lack the discipline or simply don't realize where there money is going. In this article, we will discuss some money saving tips to help you get your bank balance up giving you some security for a rainy day.

Many of us, when we get paid have our salaries already spent. We either overspent the week before or we have seen something we just have to have. A great money saving tip is to take a small, comfortable amount of money out of your account and set it aside somewhere out of site. You should definitely know where to find it should it be needed but by placing it out of site, it will be out of mind. For this money saving tip to work you should only take small amounts. There isn't any point to taking more than you should to only have to spend it later.

Remember, even a 10 dollar a week savings adds up to 520 over the course of a year.

Another money saving tip is to check into high interest savings accounts. Many banks have these and pay up to 12% interest. In order for this money saving tip to work you need to be aware of the account terms and conditions. To get the high interest, you usually have to leave the money in the account for a minimum period of time, sometimes 1-2 years. It is essential that you use money that you know you can afford to part with for this duration. You may also have to make minimum monthly deposits to receive the high interest. Make sure you are aware of all terms and conditions or this money saving tip can quickly become a false economy.

It may not seem worth it to save tiny amounts here and there. Remember, even tiny amounts will start to add up. After a significant length of time you could find that these money saving tips have paid off and you have a fairly large amount of money to your name.

Money Saving Tips: Saving Without Sacrificing Your Social Life

Today, we all want to have an active social life. Meeting up with friends for dinner and drinks can be one of life's greatest pleasures. The downside is the costs involved. Dinners out and drinks at local bars can quickly mount up to serious cash.

You don't have to eat at a five start restaurant to suddenly find you're out of pocket, over 100 dollars. Unfortunately, with many young people, this habit tends to happen more than once a week. It isn't uncommon today for a young professional to spend over 1000 dollars a month on dinners out and entertainment.

This can put a serious dent into ones budget and start to make life difficult in the long run. In this article, we will look at some practical ways for you to cut costs while still maintaining and active social life.

Young professionals today dine out on average 2-3 times per week. The amounts to lots of money wasted on restaurant food and bar refreshments. You may want to try having your friends over for dinner and drinks rather than going out.

Suggest your friends come over to your place for dinner and drinks and offer to cook. You will be amazed how many will take you up on the offer and, how the social atmosphere isn't compromised at all by being

At home. Chances are you will also find preparing a dinner party for friends very rewarding and fulfilling.

One thing you will also find a shock is the money you will save. When you compare the cost of eating out with that of eating at home the savings is exponential. Take for example a small dinner in an Italian restaurant. The average price for a main dish is about 12 dollars. Appetizers can range anywhere from 4 to 10 dollars.

Generally, a good Italian dinner is accompanied by wine with Restaurants charging according to wine name and quality. However for a bottle of wine, that serves between 3-4 glasses you're looking at 15-20 dollars. Quite easily you're spending 42 dollars on a relatively small dinner. This does not include desserts or tips.

For roughly half of this amount you could prepare a nice Italian meal for 4-6 people. When shopping for what you need be sure to compare prices. Look up high and down low on the supermarket shelves for the cheaper items. For the same 12 dollars you spent on one serving of Italian food, you could easily purchase enough ingredients to feed your friends with leftovers.

The same bottle of wine that the restaurant charged you 20 dollars for can be bought at most grocery stores for about 7-8. An appetizer of deep fried mushrooms, costing over 6 dollars in a restaurant, can be prepared for less than half that amount and feed 4-6 people.

Next time your friends suggest a night out, suggest meeting at your place. They will be amazed at your generosity and cooking skills. Everyone will have a great time and you'll have the satisfaction of knowing you're saving a fortune.

Money Saving Tips: Getting Through The Day

Today, the majority of us spend much more than we need to on essentially useless items. Items that seen inexpensive and insignificant at the time can quite quickly add up to large sums of money when placed over the long term. In this article, we will look at ways to cut costs without having to deny yourself completely of those small treats you allow yourself throughout the day.

Most of us likely start our day off with coffee. When consumed at home this isn't a problem however, the majority of us will stop off at a local coffee shop on our way to work. Although delicious, specialty coffees bought from the large chains can cost anywhere from 3-5 dollars per day.

When multiplied over the space of a year, this can result in expenditure anywhere between 1000-1600 dollars. This money could be put too much better use. If there is no way on earth you can fathom the idea of going without your morning coffee then the good news is, you don't have to. Make time for yourself in the morning to brew your own coffee. You might even save a large cup or two from one of the coffee retailers. Place your home brewed coffee in this and you will hardly notice the difference. Brewing your own coffee will cost you a fraction over the year than purchasing specialty drinks from retailers.

Chances are your place of work has a cafeteria for you to eat in. Although this food is much more economical that eating out for lunch, choosing to dine in them everyday can soon add up to serious money spent. The average cafeteria lunch costs about 5 dollars per day. If you consider 250 workdays exist in a calendar year, you are looking at an expenditure of 1250 dollars. Again, this money could be put too much better use.

While it is true that a good lunch is needed, you can save a substantial amount of money by taking your own lunch in. for approximately one tenth the cost of your cafeteria food, you could prepare a good lunch for yourself. It takes only minutes to prepare and will likely be a much healthier option as well.

Of course, we all are entitled to treat ourselves every now and again. It is when the treats are purchased on a daily basis that they start to become costly. By eliminating some of these expenditures and preparing items yourself, you could realize substantial savings at the end of the year.

Money Saving Tips: Shopping Trips

Today, we should all be making efforts to save more money. Having 2-3 months' salary in the bank is always useful should your home need major repair or you suddenly become unemployed. Many people want to save money but have no idea how. In this article we will look at some tricks to help you save money while you're out shopping.

When you head out shopping, the first rule of thumb is to leave the credit and debit cards at home. Debit cards are very convenient however; we have gotten so dependent on them that spending large amounts of money has become very easy.

You need to take and only use cash. Spending actually money sends a completely different message to your brain. You actually conceptualize how much you are spending. With Credit and Debit cards, this message is completely lost. Whether you spend 10 or 1000 dollars, the effect will feel the same.

When you go shopping, especially in a supermarket, a good money saving tip is to be sure to compare prices. Many large supermarket chains sell their own brands of items. Try to buy these over the name brands. The quality is exactly the same and the savings can add up between 50-70 %. You should look high and low on the shelves for bargains. The supermarkets will put the most expensive items at eye level to entice you into selecting them.

Another money saving tip is to do some of your grocery shopping later in the evening. This is a great way to get reduced prices on perishable items. Stores will start to mark down their items that are set to expire that day. Again, this can add up to substantial savings. The quality of the food is usually fine. Just keep it refrigerated and make sure it gets used relatively fast.

Finally, when you go shopping at your supermarket, another simple money saving tip is to check for any in store offers. Many times they are located at the front of the store by the checkout counters. Quite often you will find coupons and two for the price of one offer.

The amount of money that you save from a single trip to the supermarket may not seem like a substantial amount. However, if you manage to save 10 dollars on your average weekly shop, that amounts to 520 dollars over the course of the year. By using cash and comparing prices you will quickly see your grocery bills drop and more change in your pocket.

Money Saving Tips: Credit Cards

In today's world, nearly all of us have at least one credit card. The Average family in America owes between 10-20 different lenders, nearly half of this is to credit cards. Owning a credit card has become much easier than in previous years.

This has produced both good and bad results. We can have what we want faster but we end up paying much more for it in the long run. If cutting up your credit cards isn't a practical idea then give close attention to the money saving tips in this article. With some careful planning you could see your monthly bills start to drop at a much faster rate.

Credit card companies make their money by charging interest. Each month a portion of your payment goes to clearing the balance and the rest goes to interest. Some credit card companies have gotten greedy with the amount of interest they charge.

Company and store cards are generally the worst sometimes charging between 30-40% interests. Those in this situation have a few options. You should try applying for a major credit card such as visa or master card.

Their interest rates will vary depending on which bank it is through. However, there rates are generally much lower than those of store cards. Major credit cards generally allow for higher limits. You could consolidate all of your High interest store cards onto one major credit card and save money.

For those that already have major credit cards, there is several money saving tips to help you keep more of your hard earned money. There are so many credit card companies that they now have to compete for business. This creates a few opportunities for customers.

You should first phone your credit card company and simply ask for a lower rate. If you have been a good customer and continually pay your bill on time then they should do it for you. If you are unsuccessful then you should shop around. Apply for a card with a lower rate of interest and transfer the balance over. Even a 2-3 percent difference in interest rate can add up to substantial savings over time.

Credit Cards can be quite costly over a long period of time. However, by following the money saving tips in this article, you can reduce your payments significantly and keep more money for yourself.

Money Saving Tips For The Home

Many of us cringe when we see the arrival of our Gas/Electric bills. You know the amount isn't going to be pleasing and many feel there is nothing that they can do. Contrary to popular belief, there is a fair bit that families can do to save energy and cut their utility bills down. By following the money saving tips in this article, you will save both energy and money.

The first money saving tip you could try, is to compare prices of utility companies. There may be cheaper options available to you. These companies have to compete like any other which could result in substantial savings for you.

If you live in an area with one utility company, or yours is the cheapest option, then your next option is to try to use less energy. This may seem impossible but it isn't. Even by applying very simple energy saving techniques, you can accumulate quite a large amount of savings. One energy and money saving tip is to switch off all the lights in your home except in the room you are using. People continually leave lights in unoccupied rooms on either through forgetfulness or just plain neglect. This will increase your electric bill quite substantially over time. By switching off lights you could save several hundred dollars over the course of a year.

If you live in an older home, you may want to consider insulation. Insulation cuts down on the amount of heat that escapes your home. By adding insulation savings of 20-30 percent are possible.

If you have a boiler in your home, you may want to insulate that as well. This helps keep your water warmer, especially during the winter months. You save on the amount of water used as well as the heat required for it to become hot. Insulating your boiler also reduces the wear and tear helping it to last longer.

Many people don't bother trying to cut down on their energy costs because the fear that there is little that they can do.

However, by shopping around and using less you may be amazed at how much of a difference there is. By cutting down on energy, you are saving money as well as helping the environment.

Money Saving Tips For Clothes Shopping

Shopping for clothes is one of life's greatest pleasures. After a long, hard day at work there is nothing better than a spot of retail therapy. This is relaxing, fun and enjoyable but unfortunately can be expensive. Shopping for new clothes does not have to set you back hundreds? In this article we will look at some money saving tips designed to help slash your clothes budget without compromising your taste.

When shopping for a new wardrobe or just a few accessories, the easiest and best money saving tip is to hunt down those sales. Fashion always runs 6 months ahead of the current season. It seems that as soon as summer hits, stores are stocking for autumn and winter. This is the perfect time to snap up some great bargains. Retail clothing stores need to clear out their stock and the quickest way to do it is to slash the prices. Check your local papers for end of season sales. It isn't uncommon to see prices slashed up to 80 percent. You can walk away with great looking items at a fraction of the normal cost. If you simply cannot wait for a sale, then the next money saving tip is to find an outlet mall. Many of the major clothing chains have outlet stores. The left over stock from some of the main stores gets sent to the outlets at substantially reduced prices. You can find many great items for a lot less money. The quality of the items is exactly the same so don't worry about purchasing something that is substandard.

Another great money saving tip is to shop in the down market retail stores. Many of the top clothing retailers are actually affiliated with other clothing stores that are slightly less up market.

An example is the Hudson's clothing stores. They are owned by the Dayton Hudson Company that owns Mervyn's and Target. Many of the items in the upscale Hudson's get sent on to their affiliates that are less flashy. The same items end up in these stores with a much cheaper price tag attached.

By applying these money saving tips and techniques, you can still enjoy your retail therapy without putting a serious hole in your finances. By scoping out those sales and shopping in outlet and down market chains, you can look great without the huge price tag.

Money Saving Tips: The Magic Of Vinegar

If you would like to cut down on your grocery budget and are a bit on the creative side then you need to pay close attention to the information in this article. In it we are going to show you **how to save money on Hair conditioner, skin care products, and cleaners buy using one of the most well known foods in existence,** Vinegar. Vinegar can act as all of these items amounting to a huge amount of savings in groceries.

If you use hair conditioner then this is a great money saving tip. Instead of paying between 5-10 dollars for a bottle why not spend 1.50 on a bottle of Vinegar. Vinegar is actually really good for your hair and scalp. It has the ability to balance the ph level in your skin. It is also very effective in removing and excess shampoo from your hair. Vinegar will not dry your scalp or smell after use, it rinses cleanly and leaves your hair soft and shiny. If you're tired of paying salon prices then use vinegar, it is effective and good for you.

Expensive creams and detergents quite often make the problem worse. If you have oily skin, using harsh cleaners deplete the oil supply, your glands then compensate by producing more thus making your skin oilier than ever. They same holds true for dry skin. By using creams, your glands then stop producing oil bringing the opposite result. Vinegar balances the skin and is perfect for both skin types. Many skin care products can cost between 10-20 dollars per container. Vinegar can be purchased for less than 2.

If you enjoy a clean house, then a great money saving tip is to clean with vinegar. By mixing ¼ cup of vinegar, two tablespoons of lemon juice with about 10-16 oz. of water, you have the perfect cleaner for windows , kitchen and bathroom surfaces. These 2 substances combined cut through grease and leave a pleasant smell. They also act as a mild disinfectant. Breathing it in or ingesting it will not be harmful and it is good for the environment. The most important point of course, for about 45 cents, you can make a cleaner that works better than expensive store brands.

Vinegar has a multitude of great uses that are safe and money saving. If you have some time and like to try new things, give vinegar a go. You'll save money and do it by using an environmentally safe product.

Money Saving Tips: How To Use Leftover Shampoo

Many of us likely have a stock pile of old shampoos and conditioners lurking in the corner of our bathtub that we will likely never use. Many times the brand you buy doesn't quite do what you like. In this article we will show you how to turn those old shampoos into practical uses around the home. This not only results in zero waste it can actually turn out to be a great money saving tip.

Many times shampoos come with conditioner already in them. This combination makes ideal hand soap. The scent of the shampoo leaves your skin smelling great and the conditioner will protect your hands from drying and chapping.

Shampoos make great cleaners for carpets. It is best used on wool rugs, being that it is a hair product. However, it will work quite well on other carpet fibers. This can result in quite a substantial savings in that hair shampoos are much less expensive than specialized carpet shampoos.

Shampoo is actually much stronger than we realize. If you ever get grease stains in your clothing, shampoo makes a great spot cleaner. This is a great money saving tip for 2 reasons.

1, Hair shampoo is less expensive than degreasers and 2, you won't have to replace the stained item of clothing.

Shampoo has been known to break down enzymes. This makes is a great cleaner for removing blood. Blood can stain badly ruining clothes and furniture. Shampoo can completely remove blood stains saving articles of clothing and other cloth items.

Shampoo is perfect for cleaning nearly any hard surface. It is perfect for floors, counters tops and does an especially good job on wood. Shampoo is also able to clean your bathtub until it shines.

Finally, by taking shampoo and mixing it with baking soda, you have the perfect chrome cleaner. It is perfect for taking away watermarks and other types of stains. This mixture also removes soap scum and is a great tile cleaner.

Old shampoos should not be thrown away. By mixing old shampoos and conditioners, you have the perfect cleaner for nearly every room in your house. Using old shampoos not only cuts down on waste but is great money saving tip.

Methods Of Saving Money

When you keep part of you're earning safely to meet futuristic needs, it is said that you are saving.

There are many factors that necessitates saving and it ranges from the purchasing of an automobile to acquiring a home, whatever the case might be, it is always good to save.

The list of the different saving techniques cannot be exhausted, but you can choose the one that suits you most from the different methods explained here:

1. 1. One of the major ways of keeping money for futuristic uses is to start an account for saving. This method has to do with putting some amount in your account which you can collect at any time. The balance left in the account is used to calculate the rate of interest added. The savings

account system can be used to save money from present or futuristic uses.

1.   2.   You can also decide to use an interest based current account which gives you an advantage of withdrawing with cherubs or ATM. you have to always leave particular balance in the account daily; so that it can yield interest.

1.   3.   There is another type of saving that will perfectly suit you if a long term saving is what you want - this is the insured account of money markets. Since it is for a long term basis, the financial institution gives a high interest rate. It is advisable for one to put a huge sum in accounts like these to incur maximum profit.

1.   4.   Then, one can also lend money to financial institutions for a specified period and after this period the money is replayed

with interest. The duration of the loan determines the rate of interest added.

There are two major types of financial institutions to save with; you can either use the banks or Insurance Company, depending on your plan. The interest rate of the latter seems better; you should investigate before choosing the one that offers a better rate.

The most important fact one should consider while saving, is that, a long term saving method should be used when futuristic projects are planned, this way the money is not tampered with. Always do a good search to find out which financial institution offers the best before making your choice.

How To Save Money On Gifts

It is very important to give gifts to your loved ones from time to time no matter how tight your budget is. Buying of gifts is something that cannot be overlooked. The important thing to note here is that you should always try to purchase good but in expensive gifts. The cost of a gift does not matter as much as the value.

Invest in valuable gifts that are cost effective; the manner of presentation is of utmost importance. So, always present your gifts wrapped in fine sheets with beautiful ribbons. With a beautiful presentation, even a stone will be valuable.

Use the following tips to get the best gifts at affordable prices, this will produce a cost effective gift-shopping habit.

1.   Create a Gift Store

Within your house, create a space, especially in your closet, where you will use as a store for gift items. This is necessary because during the holiday seasons there is always an increase in the prices of gift items making it more expensive to buy gifts at this time.

But, if you start early in the year to buy different kinds of gifts and stock them all in the store, you will discover that there will always be gifts available to give out during the holidays and then less money will be spent in the process.

The best way to ascertain this will be to shop for gifts at cheap places like during garage sales, bazaars etc. You can also shop for gifts whenever you travel abroad. Keep a neat record of all the gifted you have in your store and update your record regularly'

You should develop the habit of wrapping every gift well that calls for a stocking of ribbons and wrapping sheets in your gift store.

2.   Try Creating Your Own Special Gifts

It is very cost effective to make your own gifts to be presented to your loved ones. People tend to appreciate a hand crafted gift more than others - They are the most precious gifts to be given or received. This method will help you save money.

3. Get a list of all those you will want to give gifts and decide on what to give each person. With this plan, you can easily know the amount of money budgeted for each person's gift. Always make sure that the gifts are valuable but affordable. This makes you save money on gift items.

Tips On How To Save Money

Price changes occur every other year. Prices you saw in the yesteryears are of very low magnitude for the current year. Inflation conversely means having reasonable amount of savings for the future unknown. This however doesn't mean anything dreary.

Getting to the basics

First of all, it is advisable to agree on things that are key and imperative to you. It is good to conclude what item is required and which are the ones you only long to have. The foremost thing that people don't realize is the significance of buying according to one's lifestyle.

Spend on these...

The fundamentals of food, clothing and shelter cannot be done without. These requirements are worth throwing spend at, as they concern your health and security. When means are scarce, these elementary things should be prioritized at the outset leaving the things that add to your comfort.

Maintain your needs

Listing things that you would go for should be categorized to check if they are adequately fine to maintain the elementary needs. It is a good idea to use and re use things as long as they are practically and functionally good enough to put up with your needs.

Make a trial before you jump

Time and again we go towards making superfluous purchases which we later regret. You can definitely avoid them by deciding beforehand what a worthy buy is! This could be accomplished by trying out smaller quantities and samples before deciding on any new product. This way the product would be able to justify its worth and quality helping you to choose if you wish to go ahead with approving its effectiveness. This would help you ensure that you don't buy large quantity of unknown new items and regret the lump sum you paid for! This would be diplomatic in wise budgeting.

Is it really the right time for your purchase?

It is very seldom people realize that some things can wait, and they need not be in any hurry to acquire that brand new trend in the market right away. Budgeting resources in advance is always a good notion. Conversely, you can actually plan and budget accordingly for that little dear desire you have. You can be well-turned-out by checking for season ending sales when prices are rock bottom.

Window-shopping at the outset

It is a worthwhile decision to weigh the prices against several stores before you end up finalizing one. Limiting to a single place, whatsoever the reason is never a good idea. Quite a few stores provide you with a value-for-money deals ensuring quality intact. One can always be smart by keeping in mind the prices of items which are regularly bought as few stores follow premature price changes on goods.

Electricity; that makes a huge difference

The electric power supply is for your convenience and not for you to be anxious when you get the bills screaming at you. You can always avoid such agony by ensuring to switch off appliances that are not in use. Furthermore, keep a track of your old bills to cross-check if the new bills are consistent with the old ones, so that you can get back to wise budgeting.

Optimizing your conveyance

Being organized always helps! If you know you are going to travel many different places en route to the last, then it is wise to plan and check the itinerary for the day. You need to ascertain that you don't miss out on any junctions so as to maintain your fuel expenses. Not including an itinerary would perhaps result in omitting destinations leading to redundancy, wasting money and time.

Money is essential for pragmatic survival. Hence, you need to ensure that every desire and spending gets its precedence.

CPSIA information can be obtained
at www.ICGtesting.com
Printed in the USA
BVHW041509290121
599098BV00008B/644